WORLD FAITHS
ISLAM

All year dates are given using the
Christian conventions B.C. (Before
Christ) and A.D. (Anno Domini), simply
for universality of understanding

The publishers would like to thank the
following editorial consultant for his help:
Dr. M.A.Zaki Badawi, Principal, The Muslim College,
London, England

KINGFISHER
a Houghton Mifflin Company imprint
222 Berkeley Street
Boston, Massachusetts 02116
www.houghtonmifflinbooks.com

First published as *The Kingfisher Book of Religions* in 1999
This revised and updated edition published in 2005

2 4 6 8 10 9 7 5 3 1

1TR/0405/SHENS/MA(MA)/158MA

LIBRARY OF CONGRESS CATALOGING-IN-PUBLICATION DATA
has been applied for.

ISBN 0-7534-5882-9
ISBN 978-07534-5882-2

Color separations by Modern Age
Printed in Taiwan

WORLD FAITHS

ISLAM

Worship, festivals, and ceremonies from around the world

TREVOR BARNES

KINGFISHER

BOSTON

CONTENTS

INTRODUCTION

Islam, which means "submission" to one God, is the religion practiced by almost a billion Muslims around the world. It is based on the teachings of the Prophet Muhammad, believed by Muslims to have received the word of Allah (God) about 1,400 years ago in Mecca (present-day Saudi Arabia).

The final revelation

Muslims believe that part of the divine message to humanity was revealed to earlier prophets, including Noah, Moses, and Jesus, but that Muhammad was the last of the prophets to bring Allah's final message to the world. The message is contained in the Koran, Islam's holy book, which cannot be changed or added to. Such is the reverence for Muhammad that whenever the faithful speak his name, they respectfully say "Peace be upon him," after it.

Islam teaches that the message of Allah was revealed to Muhammad by the chief angel Jibril, or Gabriel. Christians believe that Gabriel, who is also mentioned in the Koran, appeared to the Virgin Mary to foretell Jesus' birth. The revelations of Jibril were not given all at once, but over a period of years. They were brought together in the Koran. It contains basic Muslim beliefs and outlines religious practices, which Muslims everywhere are required to follow.

A way of life

Islam is a whole way of life with guidelines for the moral, spiritual, and political organization of society. In Islam, nothing is regarded as secular (nonreligious) and every action or thought must be guided by the will of Allah. Indeed, this total submission to God's will requires Muslims to see themselves as God's creatures, here to serve God and humanity.

Above Muslims submit themselves to the will of God by prostrating themselves in worship. They can pray alone or, as here, with their fellow Muslims in a public display of devotion that is very impressive.

Left The hilal, *or crescent moon and star, is the symbol of Islam. In the Koran, it says that Allah created the stars to guide people to their destination. The moon is a reminder that the Islamic year is governed by the lunar calendar.*

Above This 16th-century Persian engraving shows pupils studying the Holy Book at the feet of their teacher.

Below Children are expected to study the Koran and to be able to recite large parts of it by heart.

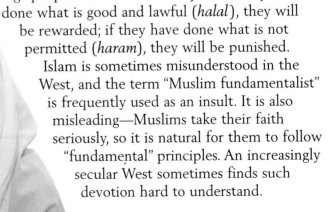

A revolutionary message

Islam emerged at a time when Judaism, Christianity, and polytheism (worship of many gods) coexisted on the Arabian Peninsula. Many people worshiped idols, so Muhammad's message of the "One Creator God" was revolutionary and led to his persecution. And yet, within 30 years, Islam became a powerful religion and later the basis for an influential Islamic empire. Islam teaches that Allah the Merciful will judge people's actions when they die. If they have done what is good and lawful (*halal*), they will be rewarded; if they have done what is not permitted (*haram*), they will be punished.

Islam is sometimes misunderstood in the West, and the term "Muslim fundamentalist" is frequently used as an insult. It is also misleading—Muslims take their faith seriously, so it is natural for them to follow "fundamental" principles. An increasingly secular West sometimes finds such devotion hard to understand.

THE DEVELOPMENT OF ISLAM

Islam first emerged in Mecca, the birthplace of the Prophet Muhammad, and later in Medina. Mecca was situated on one of the Middle East's principal trade routes, and was an important religious center because of its shrine, the Kaaba. Merchants and visitors drawn to its annual fairs carried the news of the new prophet to distant lands.

Above The influence of local architectural styles can be seen in this mosque in Mali, West Africa. The mosque is made of mud.

Early beginnings

At first, Islam was just a local religion with a few followers led by Muhammad, who believed Allah was revealing his message to him. This belief brought Muhammad and his followers into conflict with the traders of Mecca, who did not want an important (and profitable) place of pilgrimage for Arabs with pagan beliefs threatened by the message that there was only one God. Muhammad was persecuted and eventually forced to leave. In 1622, he and his followers moved north to Yathrib (later named Medina), in a migration that became known as the *hijra*. It marks the start of the Muslim calendar and of Islam as an organized religion.

Medina

In Medina, Muhammad continued to receive divine revelations, including rules of law that he applied to the growing community of believers. By now, Mecca was hostile to Medina and launched a series of unsuccessful raids on the city. Muhammad was a skilled military leader who resisted attack, and led an armed force of his own on Mecca in A.D. 630 to cleanse the city of its pagan worshipers.

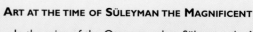

ART AT THE TIME OF SÜLEYMAN THE MAGNIFICENT

In the reign of the Ottoman sultan Süleyman the Magnificent (A.D. 1520–1566), Islamic art and science flourished. At its height, the Ottoman Empire was one of the most influential in world history. The empire lasted until the end of World War I. Its capital, Constantinople (now Istanbul), was the center of Islamic thought, and produced a culture that embraced everything from ceramics and calligraphy to architecture and astronomy. This mosque lamp of the period is characteristically ornate and comes from one of the numerous mosques that were constructed during Süleyman the Magnificent's reign.

Muhammad's army met little resistance and he took Mecca practically without bloodshed. Many people who were initially hostile to Islam now embraced it, and became Muslims themselves. One of the Prophet Muhammad's first tasks was to cleanse the Kaaba of its idols and to return it to its original purity as a focal point for worship of the one God. To this day, it remains Islam's holiest site.

Expansion

When the Prophet died in A.D. 632, there was disagreement over who should succeed him— a disagreement that later resulted in the division between the Sunni and Shia branches of Islam (*see* page 146). Muhammad's successor was his father-in-law, Abu Bakr, who became the caliph (*khalifa*), or head of state. Under the first four caliphs, Islam expanded at a colossal rate into present-day Egypt, Syria, Iraq, and Iran.

After the caliphs, the Umayyad dynasty (A.D. 661–750) took the faith west as far as Spain and Morocco and east as far as India. Their successors, the Abbasids (A.D. 750–1258), made Baghdad (in present-day Iraq) their capital and extended their territory still farther into central Asia. In 1258, the Mongols took control of Baghdad and became Muslims themselves. In 1453, Constantinople (the Christian capital of the Byzantine Empire) fell to the Ottoman Turks and was eventually renamed Istanbul. Islam experienced another period of renewal in 1979, when the Iranian Revolution deposed the ruling monarch, the Shah of Iran, and introduced an Islamic state under the leadership of Ayatollah Khomeini.

Above This battle scene is from the 16th-century Book of Conquests by Süleyman. All Muslims are expected to defend Islam against outside threat by means of jihad, or holy war. This also refers to a person's inner struggle against sin and temptation.

THE LIFE OF THE PROPHET

Muhammad was born in A.D. 570 in the Arabian city of Mecca. Orphaned at the age of six, he was raised first by his grandfather, then by his uncle, with whom he traveled on trade missions to Syria.

Early life

When Muhammad was a young man, he worked as a trade agent for a rich widow named Khadija. The city of Mecca was home to the Kaaba, the "sacred house," said to have been built by Abraham and his son Ishmael. In Muhammad's time, it was filled with pagan idols worshiped by Arabs visiting Mecca on pilgrimages. This arrangement suited the traders because the pilgrims were a source of income. When he was 25, Muhammad married Khadija and had several children by her. He became rich and highly respected in the city, but was uncomfortable with the pagan worship around him and sought solitude in the deserts and mountains.

Above The Dome of the Rock in Jerusalem houses the rock from which Muhammad is said to have ascended into heaven.

The message from God

At the age of 40, Muhammad was meditating in a cave outside Mecca when the Angel Jibril appeared to him. Jibril ordered Muhammad to read, but when he replied that he could not, Jibril squeezed him tightly and insisted. "Read," he said, "read in the name of your Lord who created you from a drop of blood." This was the first message that he received directly from Allah.

Left The Prophet's cave at Jebel Nur in present-day Saudi Arabia. Some Muslims believe this is where Adam, the first man created by Allah, appeared on Earth.

از من کوری حاجی مردم گزاسی را   کو پوستین جلو تگ بآزار مسیده

ورفروین میشو دوپادکان حاج باد به بسر بردند وببرشدند

Above This print shows a caravan of pilgrims on the road to Mecca. In the past, Muslims from all over the world traveled by foot, on horseback, or camel. The journey could take years, so the pilgrims met many people along the way. Today, modern air travel means that Mecca is only hours away.

> "Be steadfast in prayer. Practice regular charity and bow down your heads with those who bow down in worship."

The Koran 2:43

The Night Journey

In about the tenth year of his ministry, Muhammad is said to have undergone a miraculous experience. In what has come to be called the Night Journey, Muslims believe he was taken up into the sky in the company of the angels. From Mecca he was taken to Jerusalem, where he prayed with earlier prophets including Abraham and Jesus. He then ascended to heaven (from a rock now contained in the Dome of the Rock in Jerusalem), where he received God's instruction to institute prayers five times a day.

The message spreads

After being forced out of Mecca because of persecution, Muhammad became the ruler of Medina, which was the target of hostilities by the people of Mecca. When Muhammad took Mecca in A.D. 630, he behaved with such generosity and tolerance that many of his former enemies became Muslims themselves. Two years after cleansing the Kaaba of its pagan worship and restoring it to the worship of one God, Muhammad gave his last sermon, asking his followers to obey God and treat each other with justice and kindness. His aim in life was now complete—he had delivered the word of Allah, which would remain true for all time. Muhammad died at the age of 63 in Medina, where he was buried.

THE KORAN

T he Koran is the holy book of the Muslim world. The word means "reading" and is taken from the instruction the Angel Jibril gave Muhammad (*see* page 134), that he should read the word of God.

Learning by heart

Because the revelation was made in Arabic, Muslims have always studied the Koran in its original language. Very often, for boys and girls starting to study it, this means that they recite the words while not fully understanding what they mean. However, since the words are believed to be the actual words of Allah, merely reciting them is seen as an act of worship in itself. Students are encouraged to learn as much of the Koran as they can by heart, and in 1998, a six-year-old Muslim girl in South Africa became the youngest girl ever to have memorized the whole text in Arabic—114 *suras* (chapters) in all, divided into verses.

Reverence for the holy book

The text is treated with great care and touched only by those who have ritually cleansed themselves beforehand. It is often wrapped in ornate cloth and kept in a special place in the home or mosque. Unlike the Ten Commandments, the Koran was not handed over at one single time, but over a period of 23 years. As a result, it contains different styles of writing that deal with all aspects of life. There are instructions on how to pray, how to organize society, and how to apply the law. It lists rules for the structure of family life, the duty of individuals to behave well, and penalties for sinners on Judgment Day. Above all, it stresses the "Oneness" of Allah and the need to obey him.

Above As an act of personal devotion, Muslim calligraphers (scribes who practice the art of handwriting) try to produce the most beautiful and ornate versions of the text by hand. This script with floral illuminations was written by Ismail Al-Zuhdi in 1802.

Left This boy is studying the Koran in Arabic. In the Indian and Pakistani tradition, pupils sit around the edge of the classroom, not in rows behind each other. This is because it is considered disrespectful to have one's back to the holy book.

Other sources of guidance

Because Muhammad is believed to have led an exemplary life, his actions and sayings are also considered important by Muslims. Stories of the Prophet's life are taken as practical examples of how devout Muslims should try to lead their own lives. Therefore, the traditional customs and practices of the Prophet (the *Sunna*) and his words and sayings (*hadith*) are consulted alongside the Koran. Together, they provide the faithful with a complete guide book to a godly life.

Although there are divisions within Islam, and scholars from different traditions around the world may interpret the text in different ways, all Muslims accept the ultimate authority of the Koran over their lives and try to live by its rules.

> "This is the Book. In it is guidance sure, without doubt to those who fear God."
>
> The Koran 2:2

Below Some Muslims believe that the original version of the Koran has existed since the beginning of time on tablets stored in heaven. The text is venerated as the complete revelation of Allah's holy word.

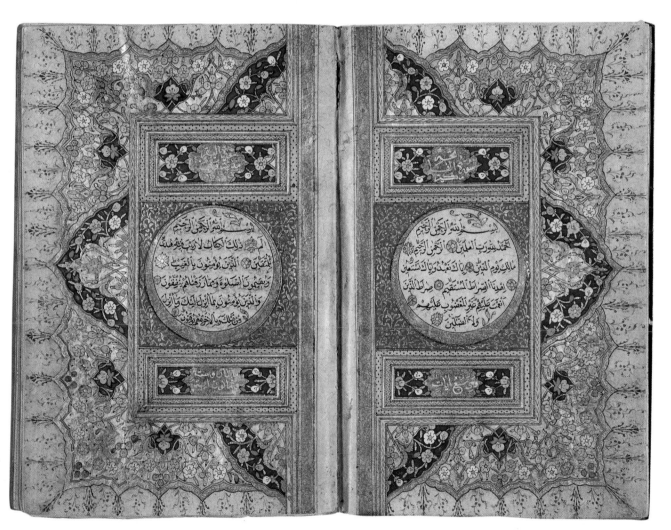

MECCA AND THE FIVE PILLARS OF ISLAM

Mecca, the birthplace of the Prophet Muhammad, is a holy city and a place of pilgrimage for over two million Muslims every year. The pilgrimage, which all healthy Muslim men and women are expected to make at least once in a lifetime, is known as the *Hajj*, and is the fifth of the "Pillars of Islam." Just as the pillars in a mosque support the building that rises above them, so the Pillars of Islam support the beliefs and practices of the Islamic faith. The pilgrimage brings together Muslims of diverse cultures and races who seek spiritual purity, and to pray alongside one another in the Kaaba.

Below At the center of the holy city of Mecca is the Kaaba, a cube-shaped shrine covered in black and gold velvet. When Muslim pilgrims visit the Kaaba, they walk counterclockwise around it seven times, reciting prayers to Allah.

Left Regular prayer is central to Islamic practice. The women and children worship separately from the men.

The *shahada*

The first pillar is the statement of faith—the *shahada*. It says, "There is no god but Allah and Muhammad is the Messenger of Allah." In reciting these words of faith, devout Muslims proclaim their belief in one God and their conviction that God's teaching has been revealed to Muhammad. This simple statement is the basis of all Muslim belief. It is the first thing whispered into a child's ear when he or she is born, and the last thing a Muslim hopes to utter at the moment of death.

S*alat* and *zakat*

The second pillar, *salat*, is daily worship—the prayers recited at dawn, midday, afternoon, evening, and night. Muslims stop what they are doing to bow down in worship in the direction of Mecca. The third pillar is *zakat*, or charitable giving. This is meant to emulate the generosity that Allah shows toward his people. It also shows kindness to those less fortunate in a practical way.

> **"I bear witness that there is no God but Allah, and I bear witness that Muhammad is the messenger of Allah."**
>
> Words from the *shahada*

Sawm

The fourth pillar is fasting, or *sawm*, which involves going without food and drink during daylight hours throughout the holy month of Ramadan. For people with jobs, and children going to school, total abstinence is not easy, but it does bring spiritual reward. The end of Ramadan is celebrated with the festival of Id al-Fitr.

Left The religious duties of which the Five Pillars are the core are taught to Muslims like this Algerian girl, at an early age.

Heaven and Hell

Muslims believe that while death is the end of earthly life, it is the beginning of eternal life. They believe that faithfulness to Allah in this life will be rewarded in the next and that wickedness will be punished.

Angels and messengers

God is everywhere in Creation but cannot be seen. However at points in human history it is believed that God sent special people to bring important spiritual messages. The first of these is said to be Adam, the first man, and the last was Muhammad, the "Seal of the Prophets." In addition, Muslims recognize the prophets of Judaism and Christianity, including Noah, Abraham, Moses, and Jesus.

Messengers are human, but angels are not. The Koran says that angels are winged creatures of light praising Allah and doing his will at all times. It is believed that all our deeds are being constantly recorded by them and that the angels will accompany human beings after death on the Day of Judgment.

Above The righteous sit forever in the presence of God in this vision of Paradise. Heaven is shown here as a garden.

Below Iraqi Muslims carry a coffin across a mosque courtyard in Karbala. The body will be taken to its final earthly resting place, which faces the direction of Mecca.

Above In this vision of Hell a sinner is consumed by flames of unquenchable fire. The souls of those already damned are pressed tightly together (bottom left) to be tortured throughout eternity.

Death and judgment

Muslims about to die say the *shahada*—the profession of faith in one God and belief in his final prophet, Muhammad. It was the first thing that they heard when they came into the world, and it is the last thing that they say before they leave it.

The dead are buried as soon as possible. After the body has been washed, it is wrapped in a shroud and treated with great reverence as if the person were still alive. For this reason Islam forbids cremation. The body is placed in the grave (with its head facing toward Mecca), where it will wait until the Last Day, when it is believed that the dead will rise and be judged.

Heaven

Heaven is the eternal reward for those who have followed the will of Allah. Heaven is described in the Koran as a beautiful garden where the righteous can eat fruits and drink juices while reclining on comfortable couches and waited on by heavenly servants. Those who have led a good life are admitted to Paradise after they have been judged by the Almighty. Martyrs, who have died for their faith, are said to proceed straight to Heaven without the need to account for their earthly lives to the angels and to God.

Some interpret this literally, while others say it is an image describing the joy of being eternally in God's presence.

Hell

Hell, in contrast, is an ugly place reserved for the wicked and the unbelievers. It is described as a place of everlasting fire, boiling waters, scorching winds, and black smoke.

The punishments of Hell are believed to be eternal, and the sinners' bodies are eternally renewed so that the torments can continue forever. Although they are described as physical tortures, many Islamic scholars argue that they are dramatic images that powerfully describe the pain of separation from God.

ISLAMIC LAW AND SCIENCE

The system of Islamic law known as *Shari'a* comes from the Arabic word describing a track leading camels to a watering hole—a description implying a pathway that, if followed by humanity, will lead to Allah.

Sources of the law

The Koran and the *Sunna* (customs and practices of the Prophet) are the two principal sources of the law in Islam. There are five categories of actions: what Allah has decreed, what Allah has forbidden, what Allah has recommended but not insisted on, what Allah has disapproved of but not expressly forbidden, and what Allah has remained silent about. For example, visiting a sick person is recommended whereas seeking treatment for an illness is required. Not all issues are so clearly explained. Alcohol is forbidden, but tobacco is different. Some scholars have argued that it is not covered in the Koran, although they suspect it is a gray area that, while not expressly forbidden, is disapproved of. These differences have given rise to different opinions about many social issues.

Above Islamic law deals with all aspects of family life. A man may have more than one wife, provided he can look after them equally—an arrangement that is increasingly rare in the West.

Interpreting the law

Shari'a deals with every aspect of human society including family life, property, crime, punishment, business, and morality. Since the Koran is silent on many specific issues of modern life, scholars constantly interpret the law, and their findings also become a basis for lawmaking. Experts able to rule on points of law are known as *muftis*. Shiite Muslims also accept the rulings of their highest religious leaders, the ayatollahs. Interpretation of Islamic law may vary, but its fundamentals always apply.

Right Young women working in a laboratory in Egypt continue the centuries-old tradition of scholarship and science.

Above This painting shows astronomers at work in the 16th-century observatory in Istanbul. Globes, maps, astrolabes, telescopes, and compasses have all been refined by Muslim scientists.

> "It is God who sends the winds and they raise the clouds. Then does he spread them in the sky as he wills."
>
> The Koran 30:48

Muslim scholarship

Throughout the Dark Ages of Europe (*c.* A.D. 500–1100) the flame of scholarship was kept alive by writers, philosophers, and mathematicians from the Islamic world, who translated many of the classical texts of ancient Greece into Arabic. The Western system of numerals is of Arabic origin. By superseding Roman numerals, they made modern mathematics possible. Muslim mathematicians also gave the world algebra.

Astronomical exploration

Islamic scientists founded observatories from which they plotted the positions of the stars. They used and refined a special instrument known as an astrolabe, which enabled them to carry out a scientific function (measuring the angle of the stars and plotting distances and directions on the ground) and a religious function (establishing the direction of Mecca—the *qibla*—for their daily prayers). Astrolabes were important for navigation and mapmaking, and led to many discoveries. Islam encourages scholarship and has produced eminent philosophers, doctors, and scientists, but it also teaches that Allah alone is the source of all knowledge and all creation.

THE MOSQUE

T he word "mosque" comes from an Arabic word that means "place of prostration." It is the house of prayer where Muslims gather together to worship Allah. There are many different styles of mosque, and they reflect the traditional architecture of the countries in which they are found. However, all of them share common design features.

Pointers to Allah

Perhaps the most distinctive element of a mosque is its minaret, the tall, slender tower designed to be seen from a distance as a reminder of Allah's presence. As a person's gaze goes up the minaret to the top, they are symbolically looking up toward heaven, where Allah is supreme. Similarly, the dome of the mosque symbolizes the roof of the sky where Allah reigns in splendor and majesty.

The harmony of creation

Although mosques are often richly decorated, the decorations are always abstract and geometrical, symbolizing divine harmony. Because Muslims are careful to avoid the sin of idolatry (worshiping anything other than the one God), there are never any pictures of people or animals that might accidentally distract the worshiper from Allah alone.

House of prayer

The mosque is usually full at midday on Friday, which is an important day for communal worship. Unlike Judaism and Christianity, Islam does not have the concept of the Sabbath. Since Allah never stops working, Muslims believe that they should not stop working either.

Left Traditionally, the muezzin *(or proclaimer) calls the faithful to prayer from the minaret, or tower of the mosque. In most Islamic countries, the task is now carried out electronically through a loudspeaker system.*

The *mihrab* is a niche in the wall that marks the direction of Mecca.

The *minbar* is a pulpit from which the *Imam* delivers his sermon on Fridays.

The minarets have balconies from which the call to prayer is given by the *muezzin*.

Left The Blue Mosque in Istanbul is one of the most beautiful religious buildings in the world. It was built between A.D. 1609 and 1616 on the orders of Sultan Ahmet I.

Above Men congregate for prayer at the Prophet's Mosque in Medina, Saudi Arabia. They kneel on carpets and face Mecca.

Once they have said Friday prayers, they resume their working day. Prayer is led by a religious leader (*Imam*) or by a preacher (*khatib*). When praying, Muslims always face Mecca—the direction is indicated by an empty niche or alcove known as the *mihrab*. Because prayer involves ritual movements of standing, kneeling, and bowing, the space in the main prayer hall has no seating of any kind. Instead, carpets cover the floor, marking it out as holy ground. Although some mosques have a separate area for women to worship, praying in a mosque is usually an all-male activity. Worshipers leave their shoes at the door and proceed to a small room— usually a communal space with low seats in front of individual faucets—where they rinse their hands, face, nostrils, mouth, arms, and feet in ritual purification.

The fountain in the courtyard was used for ritual ablutions. This is now done at faucets outside the walls of the mosque.

Equality in the sight of Allah

In the prayer hall, the worshipers line up together—young, old, rich, and poor occupying the same space to show that all are equal in the sight of Allah. Next to the *mihrab* is the *minbar*, which looks like a small staircase, from which the preacher delivers his sermon, or *khutba*. Mosque worship is based on the word of Allah so there is no singing or music of any kind. Muslims believe that group worship is more pleasing to Allah than individual prayer, so they make a special effort to attend.

ISLAMIC ART

Muslims believe in one indivisible God and are taught to avoid the worship of false gods and idols. As a result, many are suspicious of paintings and statues representing human forms—for fear that they could accidentally be worshipped as pagan idols. However, there is a tradition of representational art, often showing imagined scenes from Islamic history—but this is never incorporated into mosque design or seen in places of worship.

Calligraphy and the decorative arts

Calligraphy, or the art of handwriting, is an art form that is highly prized in the Islamic world. It is believed that the word of God is so important that it must be written down with reverence and in the most beautiful ways possible. Calligraphers through the generations have produced elaborate editions of the holy texts and used their skills to shape and color each Arabic character with the utmost care.

Concern with beauty is seen as a mark of respect for the Almighty, and in their small way finely decorated objects, such as mosaics, ceramics, carpets, and pieces of metalwork, are seen to mirror the beauty of God's Creation.

In contrast to the western tradition, which has emphasised painting and sculpture, Islam has tended to focus on what are called the decorative arts—producing exquisitely designed domestic objects such as tapestries, glassware, pottery, plates, and lamps.

Above *The gardens of the Alhambra Palace near Granada, Spain, offer believers a foretaste of Paradise. The Palace is an outstanding example of Moorish architecture and a visible reminder of the Islamic culture that flourished there.*

Right *Intricate patterns and repeating geometric shapes decorate the dome of the Sheikh Lutfullah Mosque in Isfahan, Iran. They signify the immensity of Creation.*

Below *The Great Mosque in Cordoba, southern Spain, was started in A.D. 785. The Mosque shows how art and architecture can help inspire worshippers.*

The Ottomans

The empire of the Ottoman Turks lasted for almost 500 years, from the mid A.D 1400s. It reached its height during the reign of Süleyman the Magnificent (A.D. 1520–1566). His empire stretched from the north African coast through the Balkans to the gates of Vienna and was seen as his reward for spreading the faith of Islam so effectively.

Under his rule an elaborate artistic tradition evolved with artists and craftspeople producing magnificent ornaments decorated with valuable materials such as gold, silver, and precious stones. During Süleyman's time great mosques were constructed, and some survive today as some of the most magnificent in the world.

Left *The Prophet Muhammad rides ahead of his disciples to meet the enemy army from Mecca.*

Islamic gardens

Islamic gardens are designed and built to represent Heaven on earth. They first emerged in the dusty desert plains of Persia and served as beautiful spaces set apart from the harshness of the surrounding landscape, where people could read, relax, and experience some of the beauty of Allah's Creation.

They were planted with beautifully colored flowers and fruit trees bearing lemons, dates, figs, and pomegranates, as well as vines for grapes. Water is a constant feature of the Islamic garden, and channels traditionally divide the space into four sections—in the same way that the Garden of Eden is said to have been fed and divided by two rivers.

But the water is not just symbolically important. It is a cooling element in the garden, producing pleasing reflections and soothing sounds. In the baking summer heat the garden, with its water, light, shade, and color, gives believers a foretaste of the life to come in Paradise.

WORSHIP AND FESTIVALS

Muslims believe that humans were created to worship Allah and the purpose of life itself is total submission to his will. Everyday life is organized around *salat*, the five daily prayers that are recited in the direction of Mecca. Muslims will often have a special prayer rug, or *sajjada*, for use at home or when they are traveling. This allows them to create a ritually pure and holy space from which to direct their thoughts to Allah. At home and in the mosque, shoes are removed as a sign of reverence.

Above Five times a day, Muslims stop whatever they are doing, face the direction of Mecca, and prostrate themselves in prayer.

The festival year

Just as prayers punctuate the day, so festivals punctuate the Islamic year, which has 12 lunar months, or 354 days. In some Islamic traditions, the calendar begins with the celebration of the *hijra*, the Prophet's migration from Mecca to Medina in A.D. 622. This is followed two months later by a festival marking his birth in 570.

The ninth month, Ramadan, is the most significant of the year and is marked by a complete abstinence from food and drink during daylight hours. Muhammad is thought to have received Allah's first revelation during Ramadan and, as a result, Muslims recite the holy book throughout this month. Fasting is a physical and spiritual discipline designed to focus attention on Allah in a concentrated way. It is a duty that every fit and healthy adult is expected to perform. Children are not expected to fast, but many do, in imitation of their parents' devotion to Allah.

Left These children have a homemade Id card. The end of Ramadan is associated with blessings and joy, and people often exchange presents.

Above Ramadan ends with the joyful festival of Id al-Fitr when families and friends break their month-long fast.

> "People, adore your Guardian–Lord who created you."
>
> The Koran 2:21

Daily routine in Ramadan

In many households, the day begins before dawn with prayers and a reading from the Koran. People then set off for work or school knowing that they will not be able to eat or drink anything until the sun sets. Attendance at the mosque increases during Ramadan, particularly toward the end of the month when people gather to commemorate *Lailat al-Qadr*, the Night of Power, believed to be the night that Allah first revealed the Koran to the Prophet Muhammad. Muslims try to stay awake all night and may stay in the mosque praying or reciting from the Koran. The fast concentrates mind, body, and spirit on Allah and demonstrates the important of resisting temptation. It is also thought to be a way for the rich to experience the hardship of the poor.

Fasting for a feast

Ramadan ends as soon as the new moon is sighted—in some Muslim countries, this is signaled by the sound of a cannon. The fasting stops and Muslims prepare for the joyful festival of Id al-Fitr, when they sit down to enjoy their first meal during daylight for a month. Wealthy families are expected to give food to the poor so that everyone can mark the day happily. Presents are often exchanged, as a sign of sharing with others what God has given.

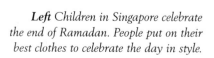

Left Children in Singapore celebrate the end of Ramadan. People put on their best clothes to celebrate the day in style.

25

ISLAMIC CUSTOMS

Islam attaches great importance to family life and sees the family as a small-scale model of the perfect society that God has planned for his Creation. In this society-in-miniature the strong take care of the weak, the old pass on their knowledge and experience to the young, and each person treats others with respect. Children are particularly important members of the family unit. They are vulnerable and trusting, which means that they should be treated lovingly by their parents, who are responsible for setting a good example in their religious life. In return, children are expected to obey their parents in all things lawful and take care of them in their old age.

Marriage and divorce

In Islam marriage is the basis of family life and the only place for the physical expression of love between a man and a woman. Although it is increasingly rare in the West, a man is allowed to have as many as four wives—provided that he is able to support them all financially and is prepared to treat each one of them equally.

Islam, however, also recognizes that marriages can sometimes break down, and divorce is permitted if both partners have tried unsuccessfully to resolve their marital problems. Even so, divorce is always a matter of great sadness and regret, and the Prophet Muhammad expressed his sorrow at the reality of marital breakdown.

Above *A Muslim marriage is a joyful event for the families and for the community. This Iranian couple are at the center of marriage celebrations.*

Left *These Muslim girls are studying a religious text in a mosque in Germany. In addition to subjects such as math, science, history, and geography, Islam puts great stress on religious education.*

The community

Muslims are expected to fulfil their duties within the family, but also to serve the wider community. Those who are able to are expected every year to give 2.5 percent of what they have (after they have met their own needs) to the poor and the needy.

Charitable giving (*zakat*) does not always involve money, and in certain countries it may take the form of crops, cattle, gold, or precious stones. Islam sees the world as a place where all human beings are interdependent and the role of the community is extremely important. The community exists to celebrate life in times of joy and to support people in times of hardship.

The money raised or donated by people will often be spent on building mosques or community centers serving both the material and spiritual needs of ordinary Muslims.

Above Islam takes its responsibility to the wider community very seriously. The Red Crescent is a religious charity that offers help to those affected by hunger and disease throughout the world.

Education

Islam has always prized learning and education. In Muslim countries there is no division between secular and religious education. All subjects are taught within the framework of the Islamic faith. In the West Muslim boys and girls are taught general subjects, such as math, history, geography, and science, but their parents also hope that they will receive a thorough grounding in the principles of the faith. Others say that religious education is best left to the parents and the mosque.

Right Family life is an important part of Islam. These Malaysian parents can offer the physical care and spiritual guidance that their child needs.

27

DIVISION AND DIVERSITY

The Koran describes Muhammad as "the Seal of the Prophets," that is, with him, the line of the prophets (beginning with Adam and continuing through Abraham, Moses, and Jesus) has been sealed for all time. Muhammad is the last and no other will follow him.

After the Prophet

Problems arose after the Prophet's death when there was disagreement about who should lead the Muslim community. Two branches, Sunni and Shiite, emerged. The Sunnis took their name from the *Sunna*, or traditions of the Prophet. They argued that as no one could ever equal Muhammad in wisdom and goodness, his chosen successor had to be the person judged most suitable by the community. The Prophet's first successor was Abu Bakr, who became the first of the four caliphs who ruled the (as yet) undivided *umma*, or community of believers.

Above From 1979–1989, the influence of Ayatollah Khomeini was important in defining the character of Shiite Islam. The revolution he inspired in Iran, and his insistence on a particular type of Islamic purity, brought him into direct conflict with countries in the West.

The decisive split

The group that eventually became the Shiites was unhappy with this arrangement and argued that only Muhammad's nearest relative, his cousin and son-in-law Ali, was fit to follow in the Prophet's footsteps. Becoming known as the "followers of the party of Ali" or *shi'at Ali* (Shia for short), they believed that Ali had inherited some of the qualities and authority of their founder, qualities that made him especially suitable to become their religious leader, or *imam*. The decisive split between Sunnis and Shiites came in A.D. 680, when Ali's son Hussain was killed by Muslim rivals at the Battle of Karbala. His tomb in what is now southern Iraq is still regarded as one of the holiest shrines in the Shiite Islamic world.

Right These Chinese children reciting parts of the Koran in Arabic show how far Islam has traveled since its beginnings on the Arabian Peninsula.

Above Islamic dress should be modest at all times, but different countries interpret modesty differently. These Afghan women wear a very conservative style of dress that leaves only the eyes visible, and these are also sometimes covered by a veil.

Shiites and Sunnis

Shiism itself soon divided, this time into three groups. The majority Imami, or Twelver, group, found mainly in Iran, Iraq, and Lebanon, believed in 12 principal *Imams*, the twelfth of whom is said to have disappeared, but will return at the end of time. The Ismailis, or Sevener, group supported a man named Ismail as the seventh *Imam* in his claim to be the head of Shiism. The Zaydis, the third group, are found mostly in Yemen. Sunni Muslims account for about 80 percent of the world's Islamic population. A principal center of Sunni Islam is Saudi Arabia, which is also guardian of the most important religious shrine in Mecca. Shiite Muslims, most of whom live in Iran, account for the remaining 20 percent.

> "When you recite the Koran, seek refuge in God from accursed Satan."
>
> The Koran 16:98

THE WAY OF THE SUFI

The Sufis are not a separate branch of Islam. They can be drawn from both the Sunni and the Shiite groups and are defined by their mystical approach to the faith. Taking their name from the *suf*—the simple woollen robe they used to wear (*suf* means "wool")—they search for a closer, personal relationship with Allah. Sufism was influenced by the ascetic practices (giving up material possessions) of Christian monks and hermits. Like them, Sufis turned their back on the world and took vows of poverty.

The mystical tradition

During a service known as a *dhikr*, Sufis use song, dance, and drumming to focus all their attention on Allah. In this state of heightened concentration on the divine presence, they hope to completely release themselves from worldly attachments in order to have a clear and enlightened mind to experience God's presence. The Sufi tradition produced the most famous female mystic in Islam's history: Rabi'a al-Adawiyya (721–801) was a freed slave who devoted her life entirely to Allah.

Closer communion with God

In the 1100s, a number of Sufi orders, or brotherhoods (*tariqas*), sprang up and were based in enclosed communities set aside for study and prayer. Perhaps the best known of the Sufi groups that came out of the *tariqas* are the Dervishes, whose name comes from the Turkish and Persian words meaning "beggar." They, too, took vows of poverty and devoted their lives to love and experiencing God's presence. Following the guidance of a religious teacher (a *shaykh* or *pir*), they practice rituals that induce an almost hypnotic or trancelike state in which they hope to experience the divine.

Left *This woman uses prayer beads to aid her devotion. They are a physical way of helping the mind focus on Allah.*

Above Whirling Dervishes of the Turkish Sufi sect spin around to induce a trancelike state that is believed to bring them into a closer relationship with Allah.

The Whirling Dervishes

Unlike other Muslim groups, the Sufis use ritual music in their devotions. The group popularly known as Whirling Dervishes rotate around and around to the accompaniment of a repetitive beat, seeking a higher level of consciousness that they hope will ultimately bring them into direct experience of Allah. The whirling is said to imitate the rotation of the planets around the sun and that of the whole of Creation around Allah. Some Muslims consider music ungodly because it can lead to temptation, but for Sufis it is often used as an aid to devotion. Sufi mysticism appeals as much to the heart as to the head, and at its center is the simple but all-consuming love of Allah.

POLITICAL ISLAM

Islam is not just a religion. It is a complete and interconnecting system of thought and practice that influences every aspect of social, political, economic, cultural, and spiritual life.

The Islamic state

Throughout the history of Islam people have tried to create a society that follows God's eternal laws, as revealed in the Koran and explained by the Prophet. The ideal has been an Islamic state— a society ruled by Sharia, or religious law, which is then interpreted by the religious scholars. This means that clergymen govern the state, rather than secular politicians elected by the people.

The religious authorities rule on everything from how people should dress to the severity of punishments for breaking the law.

The modern dilemma

The problem facing Muslim countries in the 21st century is whether they should impose a completely Islamic way of life on their people or whether they should incorporate the liberal, democratic principles of the Western world into their own societies.

Some Muslim scholars argue that only by remaining totally separate from Western values can the purity of Islam survive. Others argue that Muslim societies also can enjoy the benefits of new technology, for example, while remaining true to their faith.

Right Women wait at a bus stop in Tehran under the eyes of Ayatollah Khomeini (1900–1989), who transformed Iran into an Islamic republic following a popular uprising in 1979.

Fundamentalism

Muslim fundamentalism is an attempt to revive what it sees as the authentic faith of Islam undiluted by Western secular values. It claims that both socialism and capitalism have failed to create prosperous and just societies for Muslim people, leaving them materially and spiritually worse off. Using the Koran as their authority (and often interpreting it literally), Islamic fundamentalists challenge the values of liberal democracies head-on and seek to impose (sometimes by persuasion and sometimes by force) what they consider to be the only true form of Islam.

The most extreme form of fundamentalism in recent times was found in Afghanistan at the end of the 1900s under the rule of the Taliban. Television, music, and radio were banned, women were forced to cover themselves from head to foot and denied education, and a strict system of punishments was introduced for breaches of the religious law. The rule came to an end after an American-led invasion destroyed the Taliban administration on the grounds that it was encouraging global terrorism.

Above The Blue Mosque dominates the skyline of Istanbul. Although Turkey's population is predominantly Muslim, its constitution is secular, and rule is by elected politicians, not by the clergy.

Right Islamist militants believe that their interpretation of the Koran is the only genuine one. For them this sometimes justifies violence in the pursuit of what they see as a religious duty.

The Turkish model

In 1923 Turkey became the first Islamic country to declare itself a secular state. Although men and women are free to worship, there are restrictions on the way that they can practice their faith in public life. Government is by elected politicians, not by the clergy, and Turkish society is heavily influenced by Western culture.

However, the widespread support for the traditions of Islam means that there is tension between those who want to see religion in political life and those who do not.

MANY PEOPLE—ONE FAITH

Islam has been compared to a river of clear water taking on different colors as it flows over the different landscapes of the world. In other words, the faith of Islam remains the same, even though local, regional, and national variations in each particular culture cause it to have an outwardly different appearance.

Many models of Islam

Some countries, such as Iran under the late Ayatollah Khomeini, strongly resisted secular Western influence in order to create a strictly Islamic society governed by the clergy. Others, for example Turkey and some north African countries, have attempted to separate religion and politics and have embraced Western ideas. In contrast the desert kingdom of Saudi Arabia practices an austere form of Islam, sometimes known as *Wahhabism,* and has religious police to enforce mosque attendance, modest dress, and Islamic behavior at all times.

Above The Muslim community has spread out beyond its birthplace in the Arabian desert and is now equally at home in the cities of Europe and America.

Although Islam is often associated with the Arab culture of the Middle East, countries including Malaysia and Indonesia (the largest Muslim nation in the world) have evolved unique cultures of their own, owing little to the Arab influence. Islamic law exists, but it is largely confined to family and domestic issues.

Islam in the West

For Muslims living in countries where the dominant culture is nonIslamic, there are both opportunities and challenges. Europe's growing Islamic community, for example, is exploring ways of being both fully European and fully Muslim. They are working out ways of integrating with mainstream society, while at the same time keeping true to the core beliefs of their faith.

Right Although the faith of Islam is universal, it boasts a variety of different cultural expressions. Here, a Muslim man prays amid the distinctive mud architecture of sub-Saharan Africa.

Above A Muslim woman supervises children at a Muslim school. Today Muslim women—especially in the West—are encouraged to study and work.

Cultural misunderstandings can arise when teachers and religious leaders (*imams*) are imported from abroad. They may bring with them practices that are culturally tied to remote rural areas—sometimes these practices do not fit in with modern Western city life. Increasingly imams are being trained within the communities that they serve so that they are familiar with the demands of Western societies. The challenge for Muslims in Manchester or London, for example, is to follow a form of Islam that enables them to say, "We are both British and Muslim at the same time."

The future

In recent times Islam has undergone a revival among its estimated one billion followers worldwide. Some conservative scholars look to past traditions to forge what they believe is a pure and authentic version of the faith. Others, however, have argued that the faith has to be reformed to suit the needs of the 21st century. While remaining faithful to the message of Islam, they say that the meaning of the Koran has to be constantly studied and reinterpreted for each successive generation.

Even so, all devout Muslims agree that the message of Allah is valid for all time and for all people in all countries and that He has revealed His purpose for Creation in the Holy Koran and in the teachings of the Prophet Muhammad. By faithful submission to God's laws they believe that they will enjoy not only a full and good life on Earth, but after death an eternity of bliss in the presence of the Almighty Himself.

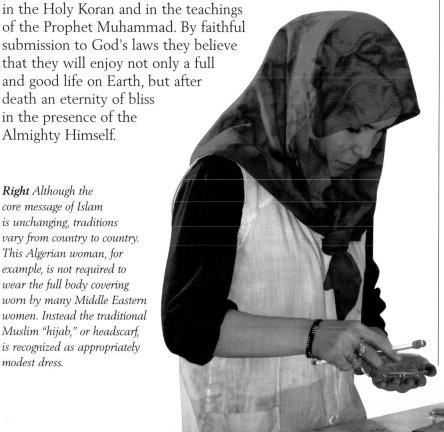

Right Although the core message of Islam is unchanging, traditions vary from country to country. This Algerian woman, for example, is not required to wear the full body covering worn by many Middle Eastern women. Instead the traditional Muslim "hijab," or headscarf, is recognized as appropriately modest dress.

GLOSSARY

Allah God.

Angel A supernatural winged being serving God.

Ayatollah A senior Shiite leader.

Calligraphy The art of handwriting.

Day of Judgment The day after death when our earthly lives will be judged by God.

Dhikr A Sufi service.

Eternal life Everlasting life that follows this earthly life.

Fast Abstaining from food as part of a spiritual discipline.

Five Pillars of Islam The principal duties every Muslim must carry out.

Fundamentalism A strict, often literal interpretation of religious teachings.

Hadith The sayings of the Prophet Muhammad.

Hajj The pilgrimage to Mecca, and the fifth Pillar of Islam.

Halal That which is allowed.

Haram That which is forbidden.

Heaven The place of eternal joy reserved for those who have followed God's laws.

Hell The place of eternal torment reserved for sinners after death.

Hijab A Muslim headscarf.

Hijra The Prophet's migration from Mecca to Medina.

Hilal The crescent moon.

Id al-Fitr The celebration ending the fast of the holy month of Ramadan.

Idol A stone or wooden statue to a god or gods.

Illuminated Elaborately handwritten texts.

Imam An Islamic religious leader.

Integration Becoming a part of mainstream society, rather than living apart from it.

Islamic state A political system based on the laws of God.

Jihad The personal and internal struggle with oneself to be godly. Also a holy war in defence of Islam.

Judgment A decision or sentence handed down, especially by God.

Khatib A Muslim preacher.

Khutba A sermon or public speech.

Koran The Muslim holy book containing God's revelation.

Madrassa A Muslim religious academy.

Martyr Someone who is prepared to suffer or die for the faith.

Meditate To focus the mind on a spiritual subject.

Mihrab The niche in a mosque marking the direction of Mecca.

Minaret The distinctive tower of a mosque.

Minbar The pulpit from which the sermon is given.

Monotheism Belief in one God.

Moors The Muslim people of North Africa.

Mosque A Muslim place of worship.

Muezzin The man calling the faithful to prayer from the minaret of the mosque.

Mufti A religious scholar.

Mystical Referring to the religious tradition that seeks a closer personal experience with God.

Night Journey The Prophet's angelic journey across the sky from Mecca to Jerusalem, followed by his ascension into Heaven to meet Allah.

Pagan Relating to the worship of many gods.

Persecution Ill-treatment because of the religious beliefs one holds.

Pilgrimage A journey to a holy place.

Polytheism Belief in more than one god.

Prophet A person who proclaims the message of God.

Prostrate To lie or bend with face toward the ground (in submission to God).

Qibla The direction of Mecca.

Ramadan The holy month of fasting, when no food or drink is consumed during the day.

Revelation The disclosure of God's purpose for Creation.

Righteous Good in the sight of God.

Sacred Holy.

Sajjada A prayer rug.

Salat Daily worship—the second of the Five Pillars of Islam.

Sawm Fasting—the fourth of the Five Pillars of Islam.

Sect A small group of people with religious beliefs different from the mainstream.

Secular Nonreligious.

Shahada The profession of faith in one God—the first of the Five Pillars of Islam.

Sharia The system of Islamic law, covering every aspect of society.

Shaykh (Sheikh) A religious scholar.

Shiite A branch of Islam guided both by the traditions of the Prophet and by the wisdom of his descendants.

Shroud A sheet for wrapping dead bodies prior to burial.

Sinner Someone who breaks God's laws.

Sufism The mystical tradition of Islam.

Sultan A Muslim king or sovereign.

Sunna The customs and traditions of the Prophet—one of the two main sources of the law in Islam.

Sunni The largest branch of Islam, who take their name from the *Sunna* and are guided by the traditions of the Prophet.

Sura A chapter in the Koran.

Tariqa A Sufi brotherhood.

Umma The community of Islamic believers.

Zakat Charitable giving—the third of the Five Pillars of Islam.

INDEX

ACKNOWLEDGMENTS

The publisher would like to thank the following for permission to reproduce their material. Every care has been taken to trace copyright holders. However, if there have been unintentional omissions or failure to trace copyright holders, we apologize and will, if informed, endeavor to make corrections in any future edition.

Cover main and inset Corbis; page 1 Getty; 6tr Peter Sanders; 7bl Sygma/S. Elbaz; 7t Bridgeman Art Library/British Museum; 8tr Hutchison Library/Mary Jelliffe; 8bl Michael Holford; 9 Sonia Halliday/ Topkapi Palace Museum, Istanbul; 10tr Sygma/A.Gyori; 10bl Peter Sanders; 11 Bridgeman Art Library/British Library; 12tr Bridgeman Art Library; 12bl Peter Sanders; 13 Bridgeman Art Library/Musee Conde, Chantilly; 14–15 Peter Sanders; 15tl Magnum Photos/Abbas; 15bc Frank Spooner; 16tr Art Archive; 16b Corbis; 17 Art Archive; 18tr Peter Sanders; 18br Magnum Photos/Abbas; 19 Sonia Halliday, Istanbul University Library; 20 bl Hutchison Library/Isabella Tree; 20–21 Roger Hutchins; 21tr Peter Sanders; 22–23t Alamy; 22b Corbis; 23tr Art Archive; 23bl Alamy; 24tr Format/Impact; 24bl Trip/H. Rogers; 25tl Trip/H. Rogers; 25bl Trip; 26–27t Corbis; 26b Still Pictures; 27b Panos Pictures; 28tr Sygma/Alain Dejean; 28br Impact/Mark Henley; 29t Magnum Photos/ Abbas; 30bl Peter Sanders; 30–31 Robert Harding; 32–33 Getty; 32b Corbis; 33br Corbis; 34tr Panos Pictures; 34–35b Still Pictures; 35tl Corbis; 35br Corbis